Simple Crochet Baby Blankets

Quick & Easy Crochet Baby Blanket Patterns

Copyright © 2023

All rights reserved.

DEDICATION

Contents

Cross-Over Block Stitch Baby Blanket

Skill Level: Easy

Materials

Hook: US size L/11 (8.0mm) crochet hook, or size needed to match gauge

Yarn: 500 yds bulky weight yarn.

Notions:

Yarn needle

Scissors

Pattern uses US crochet terms

ABBREVIATIONS   ABBREVIATIONS

ch   Chain

dc   Double crochet

sc   Single crochet

sl   Slip stitch

sp   Space

Size: 28" x 30"

Gauge:

11 dc x 5 rows = 4"

For a 5" square gauge swatch in pattern: Ch 14, then work rows 1-10.

Special stitch:

Cross over stitch: Sk next (or first) sc, 2 dc in next ch-2 sp, working in front of the dc just made, dc in skipped sc.

PATTERN:

Ch 80 (multiple of 3 +2).

Row 1: Dc in 5th ch from hook (skipped chs count as first dc) and in each ch across, turn. (77 dc)

Row 2: Ch 3 (counts as sc and ch-2), sk next 3 dc, [sc in the sp between sts before next dc, ch 2, sk next 3 dc] across to last dc, sc in last dc, turn. (26 sc, 25 ch-2 sps).

Row 3: Ch 3 (counts as dc), 2 dc in first ch-2 sp, working in front of the dc just made, dc in first sc, [sk next sc, 2 dc in next ch-2 sp, working in front of the 2 dc just made, dc in skipped sc] across to last sc, dc in last sc, turn. (77 dc)

Rows 4-60: Repeat Rows 2-3 an additional 28 times, then repeat row 2 once more.

Fasten off, weave in ends.

Fabian's Ombré Baby Blanket

SIZE

Blanket measures unblocked approx. 31" x 35" (80cm x 90cm)

You could easily adapt the pattern to other sizes. For the length add more foundation chains as explained below, for the height add more rows.

The stitch pattern used for the blanket is the Sedge Stitch, that is a Multiple of 3 sts + 1. Add 2 sts more for base chain!

For example blanket has ((35 sedge sts or bubbles x 3) + 1) + 2 = 105 sts + 1+ 2= 108 chains to start!

GAUGE

13 sts = 10 cm or 4"

SUPPLIES

650g (or 2 ⅓ balls) of Red Heart Super Saver Ombré yarn, shown here in colorway "Deep Teal"

(yarn weight 4- medium).

5.5 mm crochet hook Furls Wooden Hook, Cocobolo

yarn needle

scissors

stitch markers or yarn pieces

STITCHES AND ABBREVIATIONS (US TERMS)

- ch: chain

- sc: single crochet

Simple Crochet Baby Blankets

- hdc: half double crochet

- dc: double crochet

- sk: skip

- st: stitch

- rep from* to...: repeat the sequence of stitches starting at the star

Special Stitch: hdc in 3rd loop at back (used for the blanket edging): work the hdc stitches as usual, the only difference is that you will insert the hook not into the 2 top loops of the stitches, but into the loop under the back loop!

INSTRUCTIONS

Chain 108.

Row 1: work (1hdc, 1dc) into 3rd ch from hook, *sk 2ch, work (1sc, 1hdc, 1dc) into next ch; rep from * to last 3ch, sk 2ch, work 1sc into last ch, turn.

You should have 35 sedge stitches.

Row 2: 1ch (count as 1sc), work (1hdc, 1dc) into first st, *sk (1dc,

1hdc), work (1sc, 1hdc, 1dc) into next sc; rep from * to last 3 sts, sk (1dc and 1hdc), work 1sc into top of ch, turn.

(35 sedge sts total)

Rows 3- 96: Repeat 2nd row.

At the end of row 96, do not break yarn, turn and continue with the border.

The Border

NOTES: The border is worked in continuous spiral rounds, without joining. To work border evenly around blanket, work 1 hdc in each st of the top row, work 1hdc in the side of each row (both right and left sides of the blanket), work 1hdc in the back of each foundation ch, and work 3 hdc in each corner!

Placing stitch markers (or yarn pieces) into the 2nd hdc of the 3 hdc worked in each corner would be a great help to keep track of the corner sts to work into the next rounds. Make this each round.

Round 1: Ch1 and work hdc evenly around blanket as written in the Note above. Do not join to first hdc with slip st! Continue working in spiral rounds around!

Rounds 2 and 3: Working into the 3rd loop at the back of the hdc sts, 1hdc into each st around and 3hdc in each corner st (where you have placed the st markers); do not join, continue with round 4.

Round 4: Working into the 3rd loop at the back of the hdc sts, 1sc into each st around and 3sc in each corner st. Cut yarn and fasten off invisibly. Weave in ends.

Easy Chunky Crochet Blanket

Materials

Each 20" x 20" square uses 1 ball of Color Made Easy or 247yds/226m of #5 bulky/chunky yarn.

40" x 40" Baby (1235 yds/1130 m)

Simple Crochet Baby Blankets

40" x 60" Throw (1729yds/1582m),

60" x 60" Large Throw (2470 yds/2260m)

60" x 80" Bunk Bed Twin (3211yds/2938m)

60" x 100" Twin (3952 yds/3616m)

80" x 80" XL Throw/Square Full (4199 yds/3842m),

80" x 100" Full/Queen (5434 yds/4972m)

100" x 100" King (6669yds/6102m)

See chart for more details by size.

(L) 8mm crochet hook, pictured is Furls Streamline in Rosewood

large eye yarn needle

scissors

measuring tape

Notes

Ch 2 at the beginning of a row does not count as a stitch.

Stitch multiple is an even number, plus 2 for the starting chain.

Stitches/Abbreviations (US Terms)

sk-skip the indicated stitch

ch(s)-chain(s)

st(s)-stitch(es)

hdc-half double crochet

rep-repeat

Gauge

4"/10cm x 4"/10cm= 5 pairs of hdc and 6 rows in the pattern

Level

Beginner

Construction

The Ava Chunky Crochet Blanket is made of squares. Each square is crocheted individually, in rows. The squares are then sewn together. Finish this easy crochet blanket with a border to tie it all together.

Simple Crochet Baby Blankets

Finished Dimensions

Blanket pictured measures 40"/101.5cm x 60"/152cm.

Pattern

Ch 44

Row 1. 2 hdc in 3rd ch (skipped chs don't count), *{sk next ch, 2 hdc in next ch} rep from * til one ch left, hdc in last ch, turn. (43 sts)

Row 2. Ch 2, sk first hdc, 2 hdc in next st, *{sk next st, 2 hdc in next st} rep from * til one st left, hdc in last st, turn. (43 sts)

Rows 3-30. Rep Row 2 until square measures 20"/51cm long.

Cut yarn and leave a long tail for seaming.

Repeat for number of squares needed. For the pictured 40" x 60" blanket make 2 pink, 2 cream, and 2 grey squares. See chart for more details.

Sew squares together.

To add the border, join yarn in any corner. Ch 2, hdc 3 times in corner stitch, *(sk 2 sts, hdc 3 times in next st) rep from * around the blanket, be sure to place 3 hdc in each corner, you may have to skip only one stitch before or after the corner. Join back to first hdc with a slip stitch.

Cut yarn and weave in ends.

Sweet Treat Baby Blanket

Materials

Darice All Things You Bulky yarn (100% acrylic, 3.5 oz/100 g/109 yd/100 m) – 4 skeins ea in 30019740 Fuchsia (CA) and 30019743 Yellow (CB) and 3 skeins in 30019747 Passion (CC), or approximately

390 yd (356.5 m) ea in CA and CB and 260 yd (238 m) in CC in any bulky weight yarn.

US Size L-11/8 mm crochet hook, or size needed to obtain gauge.

Yarn needle.

Gauge

1 Square = 8" (20.5 cm) in pattern. Exact gauge is not critical for this project.

Pattern

CA – Color A

CB – Color B

CC – Color C

ch – chain

dc – double crochet

ea – each

FPtr – front post treble (triple crochet) – Yo twice, insert hook from front around back to front of st in previous row, yo and draw up a loop, (yo and draw through 2 loops) 3 times.

rep – repeat

Rnd(s) – Round(s)

sc – single crochet

sl st – slip stitch

sp – space

st(s) – stitch(es)

yo – yarn over

*Repeat instructions after asterisk as indicated.

() Instructions within parenthesis are worked into indicated stitch or space.

[] Repeat instructions between brackets as indicated.

Instructions

Square – Make 6 ea in CA and CB, and 4 in CC

Ch 4, skip 3 ch, join with sl st to next ch to form ring.

Rnd 1: Ch 3 (counts as dc, here and throughout), 11 dc in ring, join with sl st to top of ch 3. (12 sts)

Rnd 2: Ch 3, dc in same st, [*dc in next 2 sts,** (2 dc, ch 2, 2 dc) in next st] 3 times, rep from * to ** once, 2 dc in first st, ch 1, join with sc (counts as ch 1, here and throughout) to top of ch 3. (24 sts + 4 ch-2 sp)

Rnd 3: Ch 3, dc in same ch-2 sp, [*FPtr around ea of next 2 sts, dc in next 2 sts, FPtr around ea of next 2 sts,** (2 dc, ch 2, 2 dc) in next ch-2 sp] 3 times, rep from * to ** once, 2 dc in first ch-2 sp, ch 1, join with sc to top of ch 3. (40 sts + 4 ch-2 sp)

Rnd 4: Ch 3, dc in same ch-2 sp, [*dc in next 2 sts, FPtr around next 2 FPtr, dc in next 2 sts, FPtr around next 2 FPtr, dc in next 2 sts,** (2 dc, ch 2, 2 dc) in next ch-2 sp] 3 times, rep from * to ** once, 2 dc in first ch-2 sp, ch 1, join with sc to top of ch 3. (56 sts + 4 ch-2 sp)

Rnd 5: Ch 3, dc in same ch-2 sp, [*dc in next 4 sts, FPtr around next 2 FPtr, dc in next 2 sts, FPtr around next 2 FPtr, dc in next 4 sts,** (2 dc, ch 2, 2 dc) in next ch-2 sp] 3 times, rep from * to ** once, 2 dc in first ch-2 sp, ch 1, join with sc to top of ch 3. (72 sts + 4 ch-2 sp)

Rnd 6: Ch 3, dc in same ch-2 sp, [*dc in next 6 sts, FPtr around next 2 FPtr, dc in next 2 sts, FPtr around next 2 FPtr, dc in next 6 sts,** (2 dc, ch 2, 2 dc) in next ch-2 sp] 3 times, rep from * to ** once, 2 dc in first ch-2 sp, ch 1, join with sc to top of ch 3. (88 sts + 4 ch-2 sp)

Fasten off with long yarn tail (approximately 36"/91.5 cm) for seaming.

Assembly

Following placement diagram, join squares together to form rows and then join rows together.

With right side facing, begin with hook and yarn tail in corner ch-2 sp. Line up sts and join with sl st through back loops of ea layer, skipping outer ch of ea ch-2 sp. Join rows together in same fashion.

Finishing

With yarn needle, weave in ends on wrong side of blanket.

Primrose Baby Blanket

Skill Level: Easy

Materials

Yarn: Bulky weight yarn

385 yds off-white (A)

125 yds light pink (B)

125 yds dark pink (C)

125 yds taupe (D)

Hook: K/10 ½/6.50mm crochet hook or size needed to match gauge

Notions:

Yarn needle

Scissors

Size: 28" x 28"

Gauge: 13 dc x 6 rows = 4"

Simple Crochet Baby Blankets

ABBREVIATIONS	DESCRIPTION
ch	Chain
dc	Double crochet
hdc	Half double crochet
st(s)	Stitch(es)

PATTERN:

Ch 92.

Row 1: (Sc, ch 2, sc) in 3rd ch from hook (skipped chs count as hdc), [sk next 2 chs, (sc, ch 2, sc) in next ch] across to last 2 chs, sk next ch, hdc in last ch, turn. (2 hdc, 60 sc, 30 ch-2 sps)

Row 2: Ch 3 (counts as dc throughout), [sk next sc, 3 dc in next ch-2 sp, sk next sc] across to last st, dc in last st, turn. (92 dc)

Change to B.

Row 3: Ch 2 (counts as hdc throughout), [sk next dc, (sc, ch 2, sc) in next dc, sk next dc] across to last dc, hdc in last dc, turn. (2 hdc, 60 sc, 30 ch-2 sps)

Row 4: Ch 3 (counts as dc throughout), [sk next sc, 3 dc in next ch-2 sp, sk next sc] across to last st, dc in last st, turn. (92 dc)

Rows 5-6: Repeat rows 3-4.

Row 7: With A, repeat row 3.

Row 8: With C, repeat row 4.

Rows 9-10: With A, repeat rows 3-4.

Rows 11-14: With D, repeat rows 3-4 twice.

Row 15: With A, repeat row 3

Row 16: With C, repeat row 4.

Rows 17-41: With A, repeat rows 3-4 12 times, then repeat row 3 once more.

Row 42: With C, repeat row 4.

Row 43: With A, repeat row 3.

Rows 44-47: With D, repeat row 4, then repeat rows 3-4, then repeat row 3 once more.

Rows 48-49: With A, repeat row 4, then repeat row 3.

Row 50: With C, repeat row 4.

Row 51: With A, repeat row 3.

Rows 52-55: With B, repeat row 4, then repeat rows 3-4, then repeat row 3 once more.

Rows 56-57: With A, repeat row 4, then repeat row 3.

Fasten off, weave in all ends.

Dreamy Waves Baby Blanket

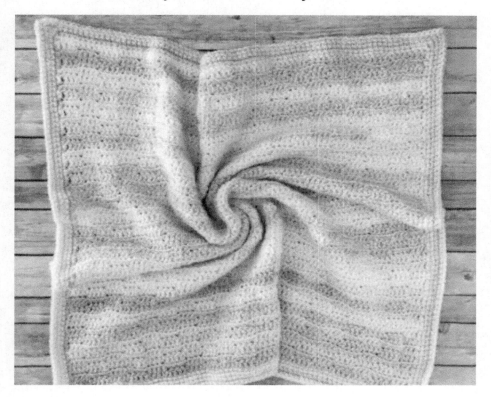

Materials

Loops and Threads Barcelona yarn ('Arctic' pictured) or approx. 650 yds of a comparable Category 5 Bulky yarn.

J/6.0mm crochet hook

Scissors

Yarn needle

Abbreviations (written in U.S. terms):

st/sts: stitch/stitches

ch: chain

FLO: front loop only

SC: single crochet

DC: double crochet

Gauge

6 sts x 6 rows = 2" square in SC

Finished Size:

Length = 32"

Width = 32"

Pattern Notes

Simple Crochet Baby Blankets

ch 1 st at the beginning of a row DOES NOT count as a stitch

ch 2 at the beginning of a row DOES count as a stitch

If the edges of your blanket are curling or wavy when crocheting the border, you can absolutely adjust the number of stitches worked along the "raw" edge of the blanket. Just be sure to keep them consistent.

To adjust the width of this project, your started chain can be any length as long as it is a multiple of 8 + 5 additional ch sts. To adjust the length just keep adding rows until you are happy with the size.

Instructions

ch 93

Row 1: SC in the second ch from the hook, SC in the next 3 sts, *DC in 4 sts, SC in 4 sts, repeat from * across (92) Turn.

Row 2: ch 2 (this counts as a st), FLO DC in the next 3 sts, * FLO SC in 4 sts, FLO DC in 4 sts, repeat from * across (92) Turn.

Row 3: ch 1, FLO SC in first 4 sts, *FLO DC in 4 sts, FLO SC in 4 sts, repeat from * across (92) Turn.

Row 4-53: Repeat Row 2 on even rows and Row 3 on odd rows. Continue to border instructions.

Completing the Border

Round 1: ch 1, SC evenly along each edge of the border and ch 2 to "turn" each corner. Each edge of the blanket pictured has 92 sts (not including ch sts) in Round 1. Attach to the first st of the round with a sl st.

Rounds 2-4: ch 1, SC evenly around the blanket. (SC, ch 2, SC) into each ch 2 corner from the previous round. Your stitch count along each edge of the blanket should increase by 2 sts per round. Attach to the first st of the round with a sl st.

After completing Round 4 of the border (or whichever round you choose to stop at) tie off yarn and weave in all ends.

Camden Baby Blanket

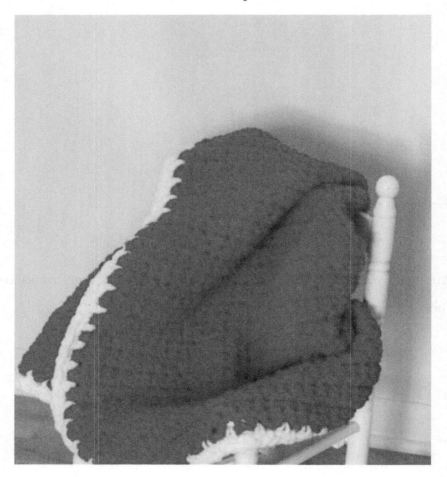

Materials

Yarn: Super bulky weight yarn

220 yds red (A)

100 yds cream (B)

Hook: US size P/16 (11.5mm) crochet hook or size needed to match gauge

Notions:

Scissors

Yarn needle

Size: 36" x 37"

Gauge: 7 sc x 6 rows = 4"

Pattern

With A, ch 60.

Row 1 (WS): Sc in 2nd ch from hook and in each ch across, turn. (59 sc)

Rows 2-51: Ch 1, sc in each st across, turn.

Change to B; fasten off A.

Edging

Rnd 1 (RS): Ch 1, 2 sc in first st, *ch 1, sk next st, [sc in next st, ch 1, sk next st] across to last st, 3 sc in last st (corner), working in sides of rows, ch 1, sk first row, [sc in next row, ch 1, sk next row] across**, working in bottom of row 1, 3 sc in first st (corner), repeat from * to **, sc in same st as first st of rnd, join with sl st to first st, do not turn. (116 sc, 108 ch-1 sps)

Rnd 2: Ch 1, 3 sc in first sc, *[ch 1, sk next sc, sc in next ch-1 sp] across to next corner (3 sc group), ch 1, sk next sc, 3 sc in next sc, repeat from * twice more, ch 1, sk next st, [sc in next ch-1 sp, ch 1, sk next st] across, join with sl st to first st. (120 sc, 112 ch-1 sps)

Fasten off, weave in all ends.

Hexagon Flower Crochet Blanket

Materials

12 mm- P hook.

Lion Brand Wool-Ease Thick and Quick (Super bulky weight 6, 80% acrylic, 20% wool):

4 (6, 8, 13) 170g skeins in color Succulent (referred to as color A)

4 (5, 7, 11) 140g skeins in color Seaglass (referred to as color B)

1 170g skein in color Fisherman for the seams

Or you can grab the bonus bundle skeins to save and have fewer ends to weave in. One bonus bundle skein is equivalent to 2 normal skeins for each colorway.

Tapestry needle to weave in the ends and seam the hexagons. Make sure the eye of your tapestry needle is big enough for super bulky yarn.

Simple Crochet Baby Blankets

Gauge

The gauge for this modern crochet blanket pattern is not critical. As an indication, a finished hexagon will have the following size (measured straight edge to straight edge.

Toddler size – 20 cm / 7.75" wide

Throw size – 25 cm / 9.75" wide

Twin size – 30 cm / 11.75" wide

Double size – 35 cm / 13.75" wide

Abbreviations

This pattern uses US notations.

St = stitch

ch = chain

dc = double crochet

sl st = slip stitch

skip = miss

Notes

Work instructions between [] the indicated number of times (repeats) or until the end of the row / round.

Indications between () are worked in the same stitch / space.

The final number of stitches is indicated at the end of the row / round between < >.

The turning ch 2 counts a stitch throughout the pattern except if mentioned otherwise.

The pattern is written in crochet shorthand. For example

"sc 1" means to single crochet in the next stitch,

"sc 2" means to single crochet in each of the next 2 consecutive stitches,

and "2 sc" means to single crochet twice in the same st.

Tips and Tricks

The color of the yarn used sewing this modern crochet blanket makes a big difference! Choose something contrasting. Using a very bright fun color with more sober hexagon colors or the other way around gives great results and really makes the details pop! Avoid using one of the colors of the hexagons as it will not look very nice.

Pattern

Full Hexagons

Make 16 in color A and 11 in color B.

With your 12 mm- P hook,

Round 1: In a magic circle, ch 3 (counts as dc 1 + ch 1), [dc, ch 1] 5 times, join with a sl st in the 2nd ch. <12 st>

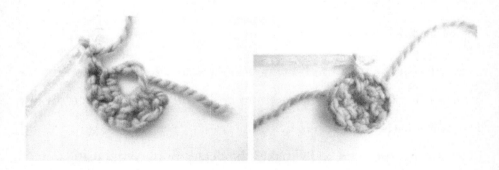

Round 2: Ch2, [(dc, ch-1, dc) in the ch-1 space, dc] repeat around, join with a sl st in the 2nd ch. <24 st>

- 1 dc in each st
- (dc, ch1, dc) in each ch-1 space

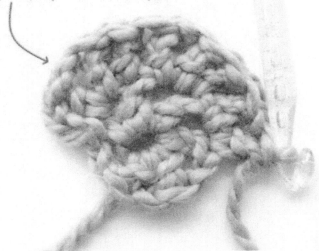

Round 3: Ch2, [dc until ch-1 space, (dc, ch-1, dc) in the ch-1 space] repeat around, dc until end of the round. Join with a sl st in the 2nd ch. <36 st>

Round 4 – 4 (5, 6, 8): Repeat Round 3 1 (2, 3, 5) times. < 48 (60, 72, 96) st>

Bind off and weave in the ends.

Mystic Ripple Blanket

Materials

Lion Brand Wool-Ease Thick & Quick yarn (~850 yards)

[or your favorite #6 super bulky weight yarn]

12 mm crochet hook

Tapestry needle (also included in the chunky hook set ^^)

Scissors

Simple Crochet Baby Blankets

Size / Gauge

4 x 4 inches = 5 rows of 7 hdc

The free pattern is for the "lapghan" sized blanket and measures ~40 x 52 inches.

Abbreviations / Techniques

ch – chain

hdc – half double crochet

dc – double crochet

sk – skip

st – stitch

Ripple Video Tutorial

The video tutorial demonstrates how to crochet the two row repeats — the closed rows (like rows 1 and 2) and the open rows (like row 3). It also demonstrates how to crochet over the open rows (like in row 4).

Pattern

With a 12 mm hook, ch 80 (or any multiple of 15 + 5)

Row 1: hdc in second ch from hook, hdc in next ch, sk 1, hdc in next 6 ch, 3 hdc in next ch, hdc in next 6 ch, *sk 2, hdc in next 6 st, 3 hdc in next ch, hdc in next 6 ch* repeat from * to * 4 times, sk 1, hdc in last 2 ch (79 hdc)

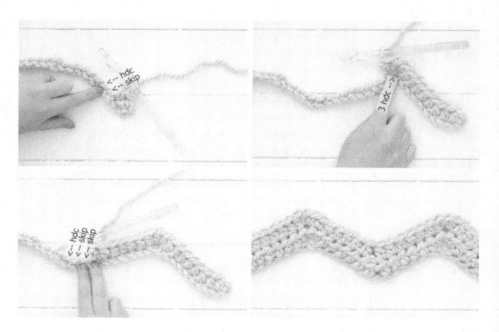

Row 2: ch 1 and turn, hdc in next 2 st, sk 1, hdc in next 6 st, 3 hdc in

next st, hdc in next 6 st, *sk 2, hdc in next 6 st, 3 hdc in next st, hdc in next 6 st* repeat from * to * 4 times, sk 1, hdc in last 2 st (79 hdc)

Row 3: ch 1 and turn, dc in next 2 st, sk 1, [dc, ch 1, sk 1] 3 times, [dc, ch 1, dc] in next st, [ch 1, sk 1, dc] 3 times, *sk next 2 st, [dc, ch 1, sk 1] 3 times, [dc, ch 1, dc] in next st, [ch 1, sk 1, dc] 3 times* repeat from * to * 4 times, sk 1, dc in last 2 st (79 stitches – 44 dc, 35 ch)

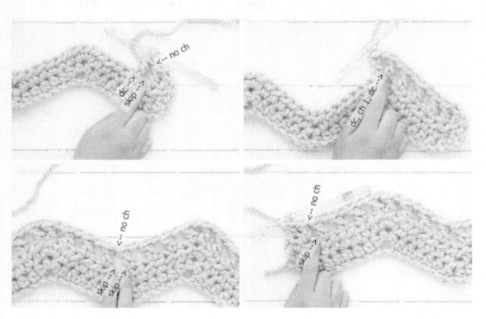

Row 4: Repeat Row 2

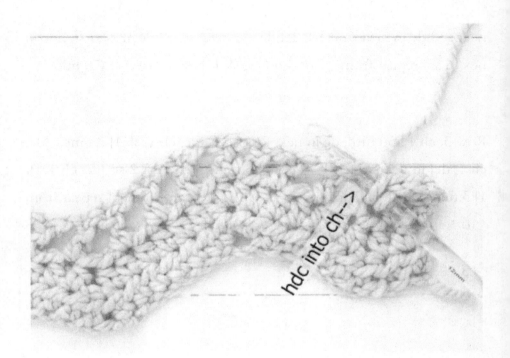

hdc into ch-->

Rows 5-6: Repeat Row 2

Row 7: Repeat Row 3

Rows 8-10: Repeat Row 2

Row 11: Repeat Row 3

Rows 12-23: Repeat Row 2

Row 24: Repeat Row 3

Rows 25-29: Repeat Row 2

Row 30: Repeat Row 3

Rows 31-42: Repeat Row 2

Row 43: Repeat Row 3

Rows 44-46: Repeat Row 2

Row 47: Repeat Row 3

Rows 48-50: Repeat Row 2

Row 51: Repeat Row 3

Rows 52-53: Repeat Row 2.

Trim yarn and weave in ends.

Granny Square Blanket

Materials

Yarn of your preference.

A 6.50 mm (US K) hook for bulky yarn.

Tapestry needle, to weave in the ends

Scissors to cut the yarn leftovers

Pattern abbreviations

Simple Crochet Baby Blankets

ch(s): Chain(s)

C1: Color 1

C2: Color 2

C3: Color 3

dc: double crochet

mc: magic circle

sl st: slip stitch

st(s): stitch(es)

*: repeat instructions after asterisks as directed

(…): work instructions within parentheses as directed

Cluster: 3 dc sts in the same ch space

Gauge / Square size information:

Gauge is not crucial for this granny square blanket crochet pattern. A granny square measures approximately: 8"x 8" (20 x 20 cm), if you use the same yarn weight and hook size. You may add rounds to each square, as needed, to achieve the desired size.

8"x 8" (20 x 20 cm)

How big should a granny square blanket be?

A good size for a throw granny square blanket crochet pattern will be approximately 55" x 64" (140 cm x 162.5 cm), including the edging.

Here is other blanket sizes, in case you would like to make this granny square blanket crochet pattern larger or smaller.

Yarn color instructions

Make 21 squares with C1 (round 1-3)

Make 21 squares with C2 (round 1-3)

Then use C3 to finish all the squares (round 4)

Join the squares with C3

How to assemble a granny square blanket

This granny square blanket crochet pattern width will have 6 squares and the length will use 7 squares. Sewing instructions are in the "join the squares" section below. Join the squares alternating the colors.

When it's time to join them, follow this chart to set up the layout and for the sewing guide.

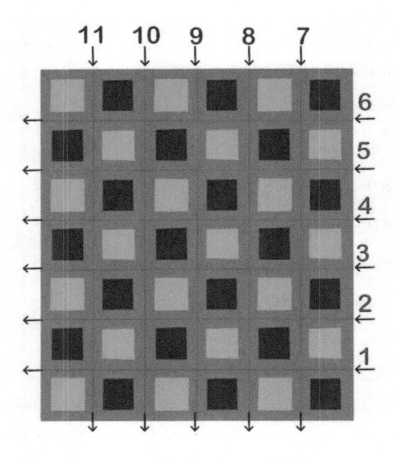

How to join granny squares with the Mattress Stitch

To start, grab the first 2 squares and align them against each other, wrong sides facing each other.

Follow the color layout in the chart above, in the "how to arrange the layout" section, to assemble the blanket.

Thread the tapestry needle with a strand of yarn C3, or a contrasting color, about 24" longer than the width of the blanket. Here, the yarn color you will use to join the squares is your choice. So, use the one you think will fit your blanket better.

Start mattress stitching, from right to left. Or left to right, if you are left-handed.

With this sewing method, you will work through the back loop only of the stitches in last round of the granny squares.

Start with the corners. Each corner has two chains, start with the one immediately before the row you will sew.

First, insert the needle and draw the yarn through the loops, pulling the strand all the way through.

Leave a tail to make a knot and secure it later. This and all the other tails can be weaved in later after you complete the joining process.

Continue this process of inserting the needle in both loops at once, one stitch at a time. Make sure you pull the strand all the way through.

When you get to the next corner of the two granny squares, grab two more granny squares and continue stitching.

Join as many squares as needed to achieve the width of this crochet granny square blanket. For this specific pattern, you will have 6 squares.

Fasten off and cut the yarn at the end of each row. You can weave in the end now or do it later.

At this point, you have two rows of squares. Once you stitch the two last squares, go back to the right side (or left, if you are left-handed) and start a new row. Follow the same steps over and over until you complete all rows.

Once you're done with the horizontal sewing, start sewing it vertically. See the chart above on how to set up the layout.

Instructions for the granny square blanket crochet pattern

The granny square banked crochet pattern is a classic everyone should try to make. It's so easy and the bulky yarn builds up super quick.

Total Time: 8 hours

Crochet 4 clusters in a magic circle

Crochet 4 clusters in round 1 inside the magic circle

Rnd1: ch 3, 2 dc, ch 2, (3 dc, ch 2) 3 more times, join with a slip st to initial ch 3. Pull the tail tight to close the magic circle.

Crochet the 2nd round starting with 4 chs

Three chains for a dc and another chain for the first ch space

Rnd2: ch 4, *(3 dc, ch 2, 3 dc) in next ch sp, ch 1, repeat from * 2 more times, (3 dc, ch 2, 2 dc) in last ch sp, join with a sl st to initial ch 3.

Crochet the 3rd round starting with 3 chs

Rnd3: ch 3, 2 dc in next ch sp, ch 1, *(3 dc, ch 2, 3 dc) in next ch sp, ch 1, 3 dc in next ch sp, ch 1, repeat from * 2 more times, (3 dc, ch 2, 3 dc) in next ch sp, ch 1, join with a sl st to initial ch 3.

FO. Cut the yarn.

Attach C3 and crochet the last round

Rnd4: ch 4, 3 dc in next ch sp, ch 1, *(3 dc, ch 2, 3 dc) in next ch sp, (ch 1, 3 dc in next ch sp) 2 times, ch 1, repeat from * 2 more times, (3 dc, ch 2, 3 dc) in next ch sp, ch 1, 2 dc in next ch sp, join with a sl st to initial ch 3.

Join the granny squares with a tapestry needle

Basically, you will whip stitch through the back loop only of the stitches in last round of the granny squares.

Crochet the edging with sc sts

Rnd1: Attach yarn C2 to any stitch in the border, sc around the entire blanket, work (1 sc, 1 ch, 1c) into each of the four corners of the blanket. FO. Cut the yarn

Rnd2: Attach yarn C3, repeat the same you did in round 1. FO. Cut the yarn.

Finish off by weaving in any left ends. Your blanket is all done. Yay!

Estimated Cost: 30 USD

Supply:

Bulky yarn

Tools:

6.50 mm crochet hook

Materials: Tapestry needle, to weave in the ends Scissors to cut the yarn leftovers